A Student Guide to Preserving Your Faith and Faithfulness in College

By

Louella Jamerson

Cover Design: SOS Graphics Design

Publisher: G Publishing LLC

ISBN: 979-8-9894404-9-8

Published and Printed in the United States of America

Table of Contents

Introduction

As college and university classes begin across the country, countless young people from church backgrounds, who have strong relationships with God, find themselves facing new challenges. Many of these students have been faithful in their church communities, serving in various roles. However, without clear strategies, some may struggle to maintain their faith and faithfulness during their college years. It is important for faith-filled students to know that they do not have to 'backslide' or have their Christian stance diminished because of this new environment. They will be strong and courageous because they have within them what the world is looking for, the power of God which brings tremendous change.

This guide offers seven strategies for those who want to stay faithful to God, avoid peer pressure, and maintain a vibrant relationship with Him throughout college. My hope is that these principles will prepare and encourage you as you enter this new phase of life.

1. Identify a 'Watch Care' Church

Purpose: To maintain your church habits and faithfulness while away from home.

- **Before leaving for college:** Consult with your Pastor, youth Pastor, or denomination, or research online to find churches near your college.
- **Visit potential churches:** Select two or three that resonate with you.
- **Connect with the church:** Once you've chosen a church, speak with the Pastor or

youth Pastor. Let them know you're interested in attending under "Watch Care." This means you're not officially joining but want to be watched over spiritually while you're away from home.

Scripture References:

- **Hebrews 10:25 (NIV):** "Let us not give up meeting together, as some are in the habit of doing, but encouraging one another—and all the more as you see the Day approaching."
- **Matthew 18:20 (NIV):** "For where two or three gather in

my name, there am I with them."

- **Proverbs 3: 5,6 (NKJV):** "Trust in the Lord with all your heart, And lean not on your own understanding; In all your ways acknowledge Him, And He shall direct your paths

2. Prioritize Personal Prayer and Bible Study

Purpose: To maintain a daily connection with God.

- **Create a prayer routine:** Find a quiet space where you can meet God in prayer daily. If your dorm room isn't suitable, consider using the college chapel.
- **Stay grounded:** Consistent prayer and Bible reading will keep you spiritually anchored.

- **Bonus:** Having a prayer partner can enhance your spiritual life by providing mutual encouragement.

Scripture References:

- **Matthew 6:6 (NIV):** "But when you pray, go into your room, close the door and pray to your Father, who is unseen. Then your Father, who sees what is done in secret, will reward you."
- **Psalm 119:105 (NIV):** "Your word is a lamp for my feet, a light on my path."
- **Joshua 1:8 (NIV):** "Keep this Book of the Law always on your lips; meditate on it day and night, so that you

may be careful to do
everything written in it. Then
you will be prosperous and
successful."

3. Engage with Christian Groups on Campus

Purpose: To find spiritual fellowship and support among like-minded peers.

- **Research campus ministries:** Look for Christian groups, clubs, or ministries that align with your faith and values.
- **Thoroughly explore options:** Attend meetings and activities to see which group best suits your needs.

- **Get involved:** Becoming an active member will help you build a supportive community and minimize the chances of drifting from your faith.

Scripture References:

- **Ecclesiastes 4:9-10 (NIV):** "Two are better than one, because they have a good return for their labor: If either of them falls down, one can help the other up."
- **Proverbs 27:17 (NIV):** "As iron sharpens iron, so one person sharpens another."

4. Stay Connected to Family and Home

Purpose: To maintain a strong support system.

- **Regular communication:** Keep in touch with family and friends back home. Their prayers and support are vital. They will have your back no matter what you encounter.
- **Avoid peer pressure:** Don't let college life or negative influences make you neglect the importance of your home front. You will always need their love and encouragement.

- **Stay grounded:** Your family and friends can provide emotional and spiritual stability. Remember they know you and want to be there for you.

Scripture References:

- **1 Peter 4: 8 (NKJV)** "And above all things have fervent love for one another, for "love will cover a multitude of sins."
- **Proverbs 4: 23 (NIV):** "Above all else, guard your heart, for everything you do flows from it."
- **Proverbs 17:17 (NIV):** "A friend loves at all times, and

a brother is born for a time of
adversity."

5. Maintain Your Consistency in Giving and Tithing

Purpose: To stay faithful in your obedience to God's Word.

- **Continue your practice:** Whether through your home church or a new one, maintain your commitment to giving and tithing.
- **Spiritual discipline:** This act of faithfulness reinforces your trust in God's provision and keeps you spiritually aligned.

Scripture References:

- **Malachi 3:10 (NIV):** "Bring the whole tithe into the storehouse, that there may be food in my house. Test me in this," says the Lord Almighty, "and see if I will not throw open the floodgates of heaven and pour out so much blessing that there will not be room enough to store it."
- **2 Corinthians 9:7 (NIV):** "Each of you should give what you have decided in your heart to give, not reluctantly or under compulsion, for God loves a cheerful giver."

6. Share Your Faith

Purpose: To be a light to others and strengthen your own faith.

- **Seize opportunities:** Share your faith whenever appropriate. You never know what impact it may have on someone else's life.
- **Be genuine:** Simply be yourself and share what God has done in your life.
- **Encourage others:** Your testimony can be a source of hope and encouragement to others facing challenges.

Scripture References:

- **Matthew 5:14-16 (NIV):** "You are the light of the world. A town built on a hill cannot be hidden. Neither do people light a lamp and put it under a bowl. Instead, they put it on its stand, and it gives light to everyone in the house. In the same way, let your light shine before others, that they may see your good deeds and glorify your Father in heaven."
- **1 Peter 3:15 (NIV):** "But in your hearts revere Christ as Lord. Always be prepared to give an answer to everyone who asks you to give the reason for the hope that you

have. But do this with
gentleness and respect."

7. Remember You Are Loved by God

Purpose: To keep in mind God's unwavering love and His plan for your life.

- **Trust in God's plan:** Always remember that God loves you and will never abandon you, no matter what challenges you face.
- **Acknowledge Him:** In all your decisions, big or small, acknowledge God, and trust that He will guide you in His wisdom, timing, and love.
- **Stay faithful:** God is committed to finishing the

work He has begun in you as
you remain faithful to Him.

Scripture References:

- **Jeremiah 29:11 (NIV):** "For
  I know the plans I have for
  you," declares the Lord,
  "plans to prosper you and not
  to harm you, plans to give
  you hope and a future."
- **Romans 8:38-39 (NIV):**
  "For I am convinced that
  neither death nor life, neither
  angels nor demons, neither
  the present nor the future, nor
  any powers, neither height
  nor depth, nor anything else
  in all creation, will be able to
  separate us from the love of

God that is in Christ Jesus
our Lord."

- **Philippians 1:6 (NIV):**
"Being confident of this, that
he who began a good work in
you will carry it on to
completion until the day of
Christ Jesus."

Conclusion

Entering college, moving away from all that is familiar and supportive can be a challenging transition, but with these strategies, you can remain steadfast in your faith and faithfulness. Keep God at the center of your life, and He will guide and sustain you through every step of your college journey.

You may not always get it right or make the correct decisions on your journey but do not give up or quit. Even if you slip up know that you are not all washed up nor have you failed God. Focus on what God's word says about you and how God defines you; knowing you are more than a conqueror through Him. God and all those who love and support you will always be there for you, God's love, forgiveness and restoration are yours for the asking and receiving.

NEVER. NEVER be too proud or reluctant to ask for prayer and/or help when you need it. No life is ever beyond the grace, mercy, forgiveness and restoration of God. He will never leave or forsake you. *Remember God can always REWRITE your story.*

John 15: 16 (NIV) You did not choose me, but I chose you and appointed you so that you might go and bear fruit—fruit that will last—

and so that whatever you ask in my name the Father will give you.

Jeremiah 31: 3 (NKJV) "Yes, I have loved you with an everlasting love; Therefore, with lovingkindness I have drawn you.

Deuteronomy 31: 6 (NKJV) "Be strong and of good courage, do not fear nor be afraid of them; for the Lord your God, He *is* the One who goes with you. He will not leave you nor forsake you."

Enjoy this exciting chapter and journey in your life as you impact the world for His glory!

About the Author

Louella Jamerson is passionate about God and the study of God's word. She is an Elder, Author, Teacher and Life Coach.

Louella has a passion for seeing young people excel and be all that they can be in every aspect of their life, especially in the things of God.

This book is written for those desiring to further their education at a college or university while remaining steadfast in their love, commitment, and dedication to God. These strategies allow them to do that while, like the Apostle Paul, also making a significant impact on those around them. Doing so from the place of strength and victory that emanates from commitment and obedience to the things of God.